The KEEPSAKE COLLECTION

Inspirational Journal

☗ ZondervanPublishingHouse
A Division of HarperCollins*Publishers*

Keepsake Collection
Copyright © 1995
by The Zondervan Corporation

ISBN 0-310-96544-6

All Scripture quotations are taken from The Holy Bible: New International
Version ® NIV ® (North American Edition). Copyright © 1973, 1978, 1984, by
International Bible Society. Used by permission of Zondervan Publishing House.

All rights reserved. No part of this publication may be reproduced, stored in a
retrieval system, or transmitted in any form or by any means — electronic,
mechanical, photocopy, recording, or any other — except for brief quotations in
printed reviews, without the prior permission of the publisher.

Design: Jody Langley
Illustration: Michael Ingle

Printed in Hong Kong

95 96 97 /HK/ 3 2 1

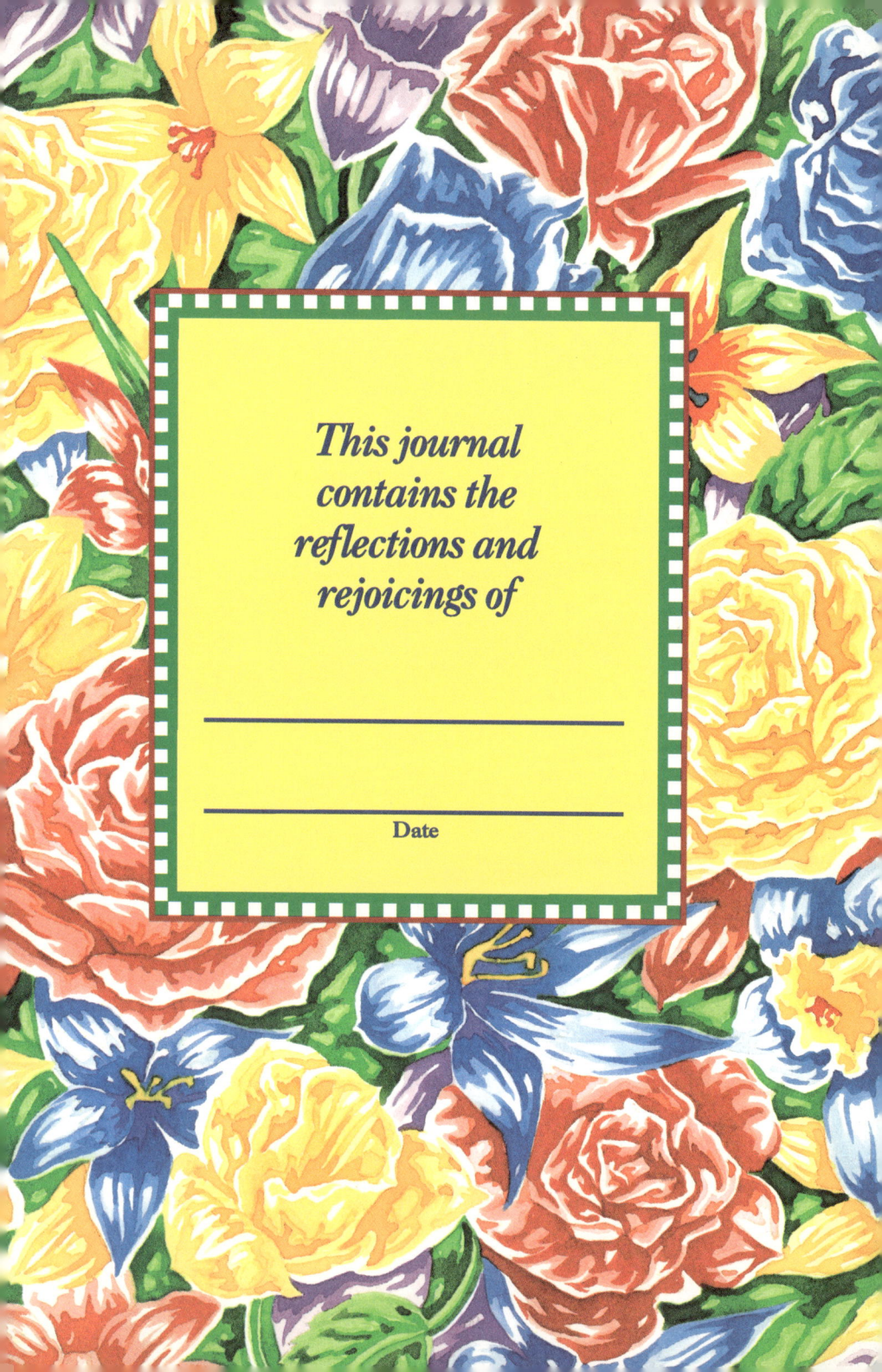

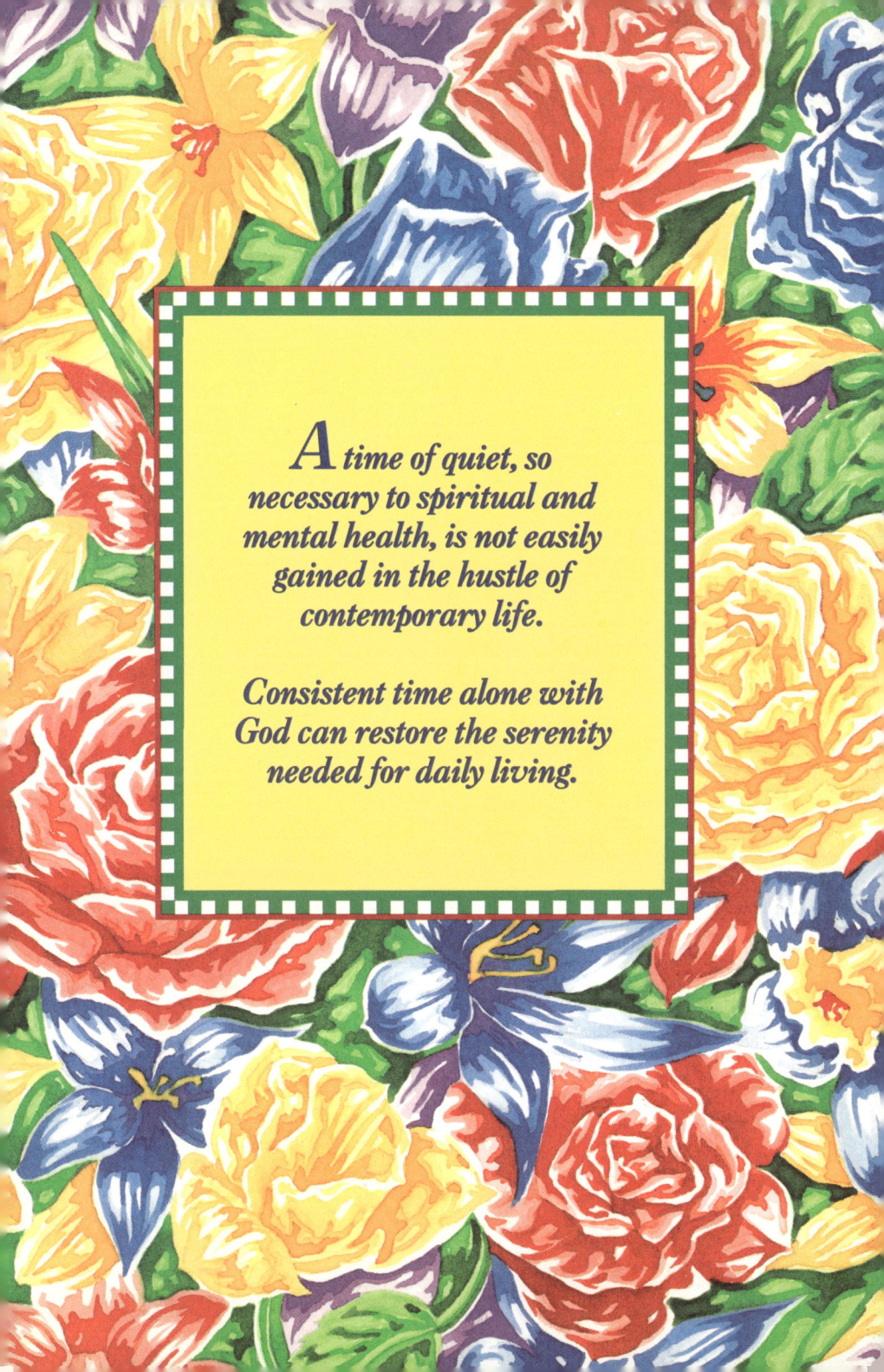

A time of quiet, so necessary to spiritual and mental health, is not easily gained in the hustle of contemporary life.

Consistent time alone with God can restore the serenity needed for daily living.

Reflections and Rejoicings

*The L*ORD *bless you and keep you; the L*ORD *make his face shine upon you and be gracious to you.*

Numbers 6:24-25

REFLECT

*This is the day the L*ORD *has made; let us rejoice and be glad in it.*
Psalm 118:24

REJOICE

I always thank my God as I remember you in my prayers.
Philemon 4

Reflect

Your love has given me great joy and encouragement.
Philemon 7

Rejoice

I have you in my heart.
Philippians 1:7

Reflect

May the God of hope fill you with all joy and peace as you trust in him.

Romans 15:13

REJOICE _____

_____
_____
_____
_____
_____
_____
_____
_____
_____
_____
_____
_____
_____
_____
_____
_____
_____
_____
_____
_____
_____

With God all things are possible.
Matthew 19:26

Reflect

You will find your joy in the LORD.
Isaiah 58:14

REJOICE

The LORD himself goes before you and will be with you.

Deuteronomy 31:8

REFLECT

A friend loves at all times.

Proverbs 17:17

REJOICE

Cast all your anxiety on him because he cares for you.
1 Peter 5:7

REFLECT

For great is his love toward us, and the faithfulness of the L<small>ORD</small> endures forever.

Psalm 117:2

R<small>EJOICE</small>

Delight yourself in the LORD and he will give you the desires of your heart.

Psalm 37:4

REFLECT

I will be glad and rejoice in you.
Psalm 9:2

Rejoice

Trust in the L ORD with all your heart and lean not on your own understanding.

Proverbs 3:5

R EFLECT

In all your ways acknowledge him, and he will make your paths straight.

Proverbs 3:6

REJOICE

Your love, O LORD reaches to the heavens, your faithfulness to the skies.
Psalm 36:5

REFLECT

He will yet fill your mouth with laughter and your lips with shouts of joy.

Job 8:21

Rejoice

Be still, and know that I am God.

Psalm 46:10

REFLECT

Shout with joy to God, all the earth!
Psalm 66:1

REJOICE

May you be blessed by the LORD, the Maker of heaven and earth.
Psalm 115:15

REFLECT

*May the righteous be glad and rejoice before God;
may they be happy and joyful.*

Psalm 68:3

REJOICE

The LORD your God will bless you in all your harvest and in all the work of your hands, and your joy will be complete.

Deuteronomy 16:15

REFLECT

My lips will shout for joy when I sing praise to you — I, whom you have redeemed.

Psalm 71:23

REJOICE

There is a time for everything, and a season for every activity under heaven.

Ecclesiastes 3:1

REFLECT

*Rejoice in the L*ORD*, you who are righteous, and praise his holy name.*

Psalm 97:12

REJOICE

O LORD, our Lord, how majestic is your name in all the earth!
Psalm 8:9

REFLECT

The fruit of the Spirit is love, joy, peace, patience, kindness, goodness, faithfulness, gentleness and self-control.
Galatians 5:22

REJOICE

The heavens declare the glory of God.
Psalm 19:1

REFLECT

I have told you this so that my joy may be in you and that your joy may be complete.

John 15:11

Rejoice

Let us love one another, for love comes from God.
1 John 4:7

REFLECT

Be joyful in hope, patient in affliction, faithful in prayer.
Romans 12:12

REJOICE

*How many are your works, O LORD!
In wisdom you made them all.*

Psalm 104:24

REFLECT

Be joyful always.
1 Thessalonians 5:16

Rejoice

He has made everything beautiful in its time.
Ecclesiastes 3:11

Reflect

Rejoice in the Lord always. I will say it again: Rejoice!
Philippians 4:4

REJOICE

The grace of the Lord Jesus be with you.
1 Corinthians 16:23

REFLECT

*Yet I will rejoice in the L*ORD*, I will be joyful in God my Savior.*
Habakkuk 3:18

REJOICE

In his heart a man plans his course, but the LORD *determines his steps.*

Proverbs 16:9

REFLECT

*You make me glad by your deeds, O LORD;
I sing for joy at the works of your hands.*
Psalm 92:4

REJOICE

Commit to the LORD whatever you do, and your plans will succeed.
Proverbs 16:3

REFLECT

The L*ORD* *has done great things for us, and we are filled with joy.*
Psalm 126:3

R*EJOICE*

The earth is full of his unfailing love.
Psalm 33:5

Reflect

We rejoice in the hope of the glory of God.
Romans 5:2

REJOICE

Be exalted, O God, above the heavens; let your glory be over all the earth.

Psalm 57:5

REFLECT

Be glad and rejoice forever in what I will create.
Isaiah 65:18

REJOICE

*Listen to advice and accept instruction and in
the end you will be wise.*
Proverbs 19:20

REFLECT

You will go out in joy and be led forth in peace.
Isaiah 55:12

REJOICE

He makes me lie down in green pastures, he leads me beside quiet waters.

Psalm 23:2

REFLECT

*I will sing and make music to the L*ORD.
Psalm 27:6

REJOICE

I will send down showers in season; there will be showers of blessing.
Ezekial 34:26

Reflect

Sing joyfully to the LORD, you righteous; it is fitting for the upright to praise him.

Psalm 33:1

REJOICE

Every good and perfect gift is from above, coming down from the Father of the heavenly lights.

James 1:17

REFLECT

Clap your hands, all you nations; shout to God with cries of joy.
Psalm 47:1

REJOICE

Do not boast about tomorrow, for you do not know what a day may bring forth.

Proverbs 27:1

REFLECT

Let the heavens rejoice, let the earth be glad; let the sea resound, and all that is in it.

Psalm 96:11

R̲ejoice

As for God, his way is perfect.
Psalm 18:30

REFLECT

A friend loves at all times.
Proverbs 17:17

REJOICE

Cast all your anxiety on him because he cares for you.
1 Peter 5:7

Reflect

For great is his love toward us, and the faithfulness of the LORD endures forever.

Psalm 117:2

REJOICE

Delight yourself in the LORD and he will give you the desires of your heart.
Psalm 37:4

REFLECT

I will be glad and rejoice in you.
Psalm 9:2

Rejoice

Trust in the LORD with all your heart and lean not on your own understanding.

Proverbs 3:5

REFLECT

In all your ways acknowledge him and he will make your paths straight.
Proverbs 3:6

REJOICE

*Your love, O L*ORD *reaches to the heavens, your faithfulness to the skies.*

Psalm 36:5

REFLECT

*He will yet fill your mouth with laughter and
your lips with shouts of joy.*
Job 8:21

R<small>EJOICE</small>

Be still and know that I am God.
Psalm 46:10

REFLECT

Shout with joy to God, all the earth!
Psalm 66:1

Rejoice

May you be blessed by the LORD, the Maker of heaven and earth.
Psalm 115:15

REFLECT

*May the righteous be glad and rejoice before God;
may they be happy and joyful.*

Psalm 68:3

REJOICE

The LORD your God will bless you in all your harvest and in all the work of your hands, and your joy will be complete.

Deuteronomy 16:15

REFLECT

My lips will shout for joy when I sing praise to you — I, whom you have redeemed.

Psalm 71:23

REJOICE

There is a time for everything, and a season for every activity under heaven.

Ecclesiastes 3:1

R<small>EFLECT</small>

*Rejoice in the L*ORD*, you who are righteous, and praise his holy name.*
Psalm 97:12

REJOICE

O LORD, our Lord, how majestic is your name in all the earth!
Psalm 8:9

REFLECT

The fruit of the Spirit is love, joy, peace, patience, kindness, goodness, faithfulness, gentleness and self-control.
Galatians 5:22

REJOICE

The heavens declare the glory of God.
Psalm 19:1

REFLECT

I have told you this so that my joy may be in you and that your joy may be complete.

John 15:11

REJOICE

Let us love one another, for love comes from God.
1 John 4:7

REFLECT

Be joyful in hope, patient in affliction, faithful in prayer.
Romans 12:12

Rejoice

*How many are your works, O LORD!
In wisdom you made them all.*

Psalm 104:24

REFLECT

Be joyful always.
1 Thessalonians 5:16

Rejoice

He has made everything beautiful in its time.
Ecclesiastes 3:11

REFLECT

Rejoice in the Lord always. I will say it again: Rejoice!
Philippians 4:4

R EJOICE

The grace of the Lord Jesus be with you.
1 Corinthians 16:23

REFLECT

Yet I will rejoice in the LORD, I will be joyful in God my Savior.
Habakkuk 3:18

REJOICE

In his heart a man plans his course, but the LORD determines his steps.

Proverbs 16:9

REFLECT

*You make me glad by your deeds, O LORD;
I sing for joy at the works of your hands.*

Psalm 92:4

REJOICE

Commit to the LORD whatever you do, and your plans will succeed.
Proverbs 16:3

REFLECT

The LORD has done great things for us, and we are filled with joy.
Psalm 126:3

REJOICE

The earth is full of his unfailing love.
Psalm 33:5

Reflect

We rejoice in the hope of the glory of God.
Romans 5:2

R<small>EJOICE</small>

Be exalted, O God, above the heavens; let your glory be over all the earth.

Psalm 57:5

Reflect

Be glad and rejoice forever in what I will create.
Isaiah 65:18

Rejoice

Listen to advise and accept instruction and in the end you will be wise.

Proverbs 19:20

Reflect

You will go out in joy and be led forth in peace.
Isaiah 55:12

Rejoice

He makes me lie down in green pastures, he leads me beside quiet waters.
Psalm 23:2

Reflect

I will sing and make music to the LORD.
Psalm 27:6

REJOICE

I will send down showers in season; there will be showers of blessing.
Ezekial 34:26

REFLECT

Sing joyfully to the LORD, you righteous; it is fitting for the upright to praise him.

Psalm 33:1

REJOICE

Every good and perfect gift is from above, coming down from the Father of the heavenly lights.

James 1:17

REFLECT

Clap your hands, all you nations; shout to God with cries of joy.
Psalm 47:1

Rejoice

Do not boast about tomorrow, for you do not know what a day may bring forth.

Proverbs 27:1

Reflect

Let the heavens rejoice, let the earth be glad; let the sea resound, and all that is in it.

Psalm 96:11

Rejoice

As for God, his way is perfect.
Psalm 18:30

Reflect

A friend loves at all times.
Proverbs 17:17

REJOICE

Cast all your anxiety on him because he cares for you.
1 Peter 5:7

REFLECT

For great is his love toward us, and the faithfulness of the LORD endures forever.

Psalm 117:2

REJOICE

Delight yourself in the LORD and he will give you the desires of your heart.
Psalm 37:4

REFLECT

I will be glad and rejoice in you.
Psalm 9:2

Rejoice

*Trust in the L*ORD *with all your heart and lean not on your own understanding.*

Proverbs 3:5

REFLECT

In all your ways acknowledge him and he will make your paths straight.

Proverbs 3:6

R<small>EJOICE</small>

Your love, O LORD reaches to the heavens, your faithfulness to the skies.

Psalm 36:5

REFLECT

*He will yet fill your mouth with laughter and
your lips with shouts of joy.*
Job 8:21

REJOICE

Be still and know that I am God.
Psalm 46:10

REFLECT

Shout with joy to God, all the earth!
Psalm 66:1

Rejoice

May you be blessed by the LORD, the Maker of heaven and earth.
Psalm 115:15

REFLECT

*May the righteous be glad and rejoice before God;
may they be happy and joyful.*

Psalm 68:3

R<small>EJOICE</small>

The LORD your God will bless you in all your harvest and in all the work of your hands, and your joy will be complete.

Deuteronomy 16:15

REFLECT

My lips will shout for joy when I sing praise to you — I, whom you have redeemed.

Psalm 71:23

REJOICE

There is a time for everything, and a season for every activity under heaven.

Ecclesiastes 3:1

Reflect

Rejoice in the LORD, you who are righteous, and praise his holy name.

Psalm 97:12

REJOICE

O LORD, our Lord, how majestic is your name in all the earth!
Psalm 8:9

REFLECT

The fruit of the Spirit is love, joy, peace, patience, kindness, goodness, faithfulness, gentleness and self-control.

Galatians 5:22

REJOICE

The heavens declare the glory of God.
Psalm 19:1

Reflect

I have told you this so that my joy may be in you and that your joy may be complete.

John 15:11

REJOICE

Let us love one another, for love comes from God.
1 John 4:7

REFLECT

Be joyful in hope, patient in affliction, faithful in prayer.
Romans 12:12

REJOICE

*How many are your works, O LORD!
In wisdom you made them all.*

Psalm 104:24

REFLECT

Be joyful always.
1 Thessalonians 5:16

REJOICE

He has made everything beautiful in its time.
Ecclesiastes 3:11

REFLECT

Rejoice in the Lord always. I will say it again: Rejoice!
Philippians 4:4

REJOICE

The grace of the Lord Jesus be with you.
1 Corinthians 16:23

REFLECT

*Yet I will rejoice in the L*ORD*, I will be joyful in God my Savior.*
Habakkuk 3:18

R<small>EJOICE</small>

In his heart a man plans his course, but the LORD determines his steps.

Proverbs 16:9

REFLECT

*You make me glad by your deeds, O LORD;
I sing for joy at the works of your hands.*
Psalm 92:4

REJOICE

Commit to the LORD whatever you do, and your plans will succeed.
Proverbs 16:3

REFLECT

*The L**ORD** has done great things for us, and we are filled with joy.*
Psalm 126:3

R EJOICE

The earth is full of his unfailing love.
Psalm 33:5

Reflect

We rejoice in the hope of the glory of God.
Romans 5:2

REJOICE

Be exalted, O God, above the heavens; let your glory be over all the earth.

Psalm 57:5

REFLECT

Be glad and rejoice forever in what I will create.
Isaiah 65:18

REJOICE

Listen to advise and accept instruction and in the end you will be wise.

Proverbs 19:20

REFLECT

You will go out in joy and be led forth in peace.
Isaiah 55:12

REJOICE

He makes me lie down in green pastures, he leads me beside quiet waters.
Psalm 23:2

Reflect

I will sing and make music to the LORD.
Psalm 27:6

REJOICE

I will send down showers in season; there will be showers of blessing.
Ezekial 34:26

Reflect

Sing joyfully to the LORD, you righteous; it is fitting for the upright to praise him.

Psalm 33:1

REJOICE

Every good and perfect gift is from above, coming down from the Father of the heavenly lights.

James 1:17

Reflect

Clap your hands, all you nations; shout to God with cries of joy.
Psalm 47:1

R<small>EJOICE</small>

Do not boast about tomorrow, for you do not know what a day may bring forth.

Proverbs 27:1

Reflect

Let the heavens rejoice, let the earth be glad; let the sea resound, and all that is in it.

Psalm 96:11

REJOICE